Oscar® winner Emma Stone gets their Oscar® engraved at the Governors Ball following the live ABC telecast of the 96th Oscars® at the Dolby® Theatre at Ovation Hollywood in Los Angeles, CA, on Sunday, March 10, 2024. Photo Credit: Blaine Ohigashi / ©A.M.P.A.S.

PHOTO CREDIT: STUDIO CRBN

IMAGINE

Imagine is a design studio founded in 2014 by French interior designer Mélodie Violet. Specializing in high-end major renovations, Imagine conceptualizes and designs environments noted for their simplicity, balance, and timelessness in Paris, Montreal, and the French Riviera.

Editor's Note

Dear Readers,

Welcome to the 46th issue of VMH Magazine! We are thrilled to bring you an issue that is all about discovering one's greatness and the power within. In this issue, we delve deep into the concept of removing self-imposed limitations to unleash your full potential and achieve greatness. We believe that everyone has the power within them to accomplish extraordinary things, and we hope that this issue will inspire you to break free from any self-imposed barriers and reach for the stars.

In addition to our main feature, we have an array of exciting content to offer. We are delighted to bring you highlights from the 96th Oscars awards ceremony, where we celebrate the incredible talents and creativity that bring stories to life on the big screen. The Oscars are a celebration of artistic achievement, and we are thrilled to share the magic of this prestigious event with you.

Furthermore, we understand the importance of self-care and self-love in the journey towards greatness. That's why we have included tips for being kinder to ourselves in this issue. We believe that nurturing our well-being is essential for achieving our full potential, and we hope that these tips will resonate with you.

One of the highlights of this issue is the inspiring success story of culinary maestro Wolfgang Puck. Wolfgang's journey from Europe to the United States, and his rise to fame as a

renowned chef catering to the Hollywood elite, is nothing short of remarkable.

His story serves as a testament to the power of hard work, passion, and perseverance, and we are honored to share it with you.

As you immerse yourself in this issue, we encourage you to embrace the message of discovering your greatness and the power within. We hope that the stories, features, and insights within these pages will ignite a spark within you, motivating you to pursue your dreams and live your best life.

Thank you for joining us for another exciting issue of VMH Magazine. We hope you find inspiration, motivation, and empowerment within these pages.

Best wishes,

Vikki Jones

Editor-in-Chief

Table of Contents

Cover Image: Vikki Jones
Photography Credit: Garry Jones

The Governors Ball Press Preview for the 96th Oscars® at Ovation Hollywood on Tuesday, March 5, 2024. The 96th Oscars will air on Sunday, March 10, 2024 live on ABC. Credit: Richard Harbaugh / ©A.M.P.A.S.

Keke Palmer attends the 55th NAACP Image Awards at Shrine Auditorium and Expo Hall on March 16, 2024 in Los Angeles, California. (Photo by Paras Griffin/Getty Images for BET)

Usher accepts the "Entertainer of the Year" award onstage during the 55th NAACP Image Awards at Shrine Auditorium and Expo Hall on March 16, 2024 in Los Angeles, California. (Photo by Paras Griffin/Getty Images for BET)

Taraji P. Henson attends the 55th NAACP Image Awards at Shrine Auditorium and Expo Hall on March 16, 2024 in Los Angeles, California. (Photo by Paras Griffin/Getty Images for BET)

DDG and Halle Bailey attend the 55th NAACP Image Awards at Shrine Auditorium and Expo Hall on March 16, 2024 in Los Angeles, California. (Photo by Arturo Holmes/Getty Images for BET)

Tisha Campbell, Taraji P. Henson and Angela Bassett attend the 55th NAACP Image Awards at Shrine Auditorium and Expo Hall on March 16, 2024 in Los Angeles, California. (Photo by Johnny Nunez/Getty Images for BET)

The "55th Image Awards" were filled with memorable moments as the NAACP honored exceptional talent and achievements. The stage was also graced by Amanda Gorman, who delivered a powerful poetic speech upon receiving the Chairman's Award, presented by NAACP Chairman Leon Russell. Usher, Fantasia Barrino, and the

Queen Latifah speaks onstage during the 55th NAACP Image Awards at Shrine Auditorium and Expo Hall on March 16, 2024 in Los Angeles, California. (Photo by Paras Griffin/Getty Images for BET)

cast of The Color Purple also made their mark on the stage, showcasing their exceptional talents and contributions to the entertainment industry. The night ended on a high note with Usher receiving the prestigious Entertainer of the Year award, presented by none other than Oprah Winfrey in a surprise appearance.

Fantasia Barrino accepts the Outstanding Actress in a Motion Picture award for "The Color Purple" onstage during the 55th NAACP Image Awards at Shrine Auditorium and Expo Hall on March 16, 2024 in Los Angeles, California. (Photo by Aaron J. Thornton/Getty Images for BET)

Oprah Winfrey speaks onstage during the 55th NAACP Image Awards at Shrine Auditorium and Expo Hall on March 16, 2024 in Los Angeles, California. (Photo by Paras Griffin/Getty Images for BET)

BE KIND TO YOURSELF

Written by Vikki Jones

We often set high expectations, push ourselves to the limit, and criticize our perceived shortcomings. However, there is a transformative power in being kinder to oneself, and it starts with practicing self-compassion. By fostering a mindset of kindness and understanding towards ourselves, we can significantly improve our emotional well-being, maintain healthy boundaries, and prioritize self-care.

Self-compassion encourages individuals to become more attuned to their emotional needs and limits. It enables us to recognize when we are feeling overwhelmed or stressed, and to take the necessary steps to address those feelings. This heightened self-awareness empowers individuals to set clear boundaries, say no to additional responsibilities when needed, and safeguard their emotional well-being.

Moreover, self-compassion nurtures the courage to prioritize our own well-being. It reduces the likelihood of succumbing to unrealistic standards and taking on too much, as individuals become more comfortable with setting limits and recognizing their capacity. By embracing self-compassion, we empower ourselves to establish clear boundaries and honor our emotional needs.

The practice of self-compassion empowers individuals to recognize and respect their emotional boundaries, prioritize self-care, and maintain a healthy balance in their lives.

In addition, self-compassion is a catalyst for self-care. By being kind and understanding towards ourselves, we are more likely to engage in activities that promote well-being and rejuvenation. This includes prioritizing activities that bring joy, relaxation, and rejuvenation, thus contributing to maintaining emotional boundaries and a healthy balance in life.

Furthermore, practicing self-compassion enhances emotional resilience. It equips individuals with the ability to bounce back from setbacks and challenges. This resilience allows us to maintain emotional boundaries even in the face of external pressures or demands, as we become better able to recognize and address our emotional needs.

PRIORITIZE
SELF CARE
GUIDE & WORKBOOK

WRITTEN BY
VIKKI JONES
BARNES&NOBLE
BOOKSELLERS
amazon.com

In essence, the practice of self-compassion empowers individuals to recognize and respect their emotional boundaries, prioritize self-care, and maintain a healthy balance in their lives. By fostering self-awareness, encouraging the setting of boundaries, promoting self-care, and enhancing emotional resilience, self-compassion plays a crucial role in supporting emotional well-being.

Setting clear boundaries is essential for prioritizing self-care and adhering to emotional boundaries in daily life. This involves communicating your limits to others and being assertive about what you can and cannot take on. It may mean saying no to additional responsibilities when you're already feeling overwhelmed, or recognizing when it's time to step back and take a break.

Prioritizing rest and relaxation: Getting adequate sleep, taking breaks during the day, and scheduling downtime are important for preventing burnout.

Establishing a self-care routine is also crucial. This routine might include activities such as exercise, meditation, reading, or spending time with loved ones. Making time for activities that bring joy and relaxation is vital for maintaining emotional well-being. By incorporating these activities into their daily lives, individuals can ensure that they are consistently taking care of their emotional health.

Learning to recognize and manage stress is another important aspect of prioritizing self-care. It's crucial to identify the signs of stress and take steps to manage it. This might involve taking breaks when needed, practicing deep breathing, or seeking professional help if necessary. Managing stress is key to preventing emotional burnout and maintaining a healthy balance in daily life.

Prioritizing rest and relaxation is also essential. Getting adequate sleep, taking breaks during the day, and scheduling downtime are important for recharging and preventing burnout. By making time for rest and relaxation, individuals can ensure that they are taking care of their emotional well-being and avoiding the negative effects of chronic stress and exhaustion.

Seeking support is another practical way to prioritize self-care and adhere to emotional boundaries. Surrounding yourself with a strong support system and reaching out for help when needed is essential. This could involve talking to friends, family, or a therapist about your emotional needs. Having a support system in place can provide comfort and guidance during challenging times, and can help individuals maintain their emotional boundaries.

Finally, practicing self-compassion is crucial. Being kind to yourself, forgiving your mistakes, and acknowledging your efforts are essential for maintaining emotional boundaries and prioritizing self-care. By treating themselves with kindness and understanding, individuals can ensure that they are consistently taking care of their emotional well-being.

RECAP: Practical ways to prioritize self-care and adhere emotional boundaries in their daily lives:

1. Setting clear boundaries: This involves communicating your limits to others and being assertive about what you can and cannot take on. This might mean saying no to additional responsibilities when you're already feeling overwhelmed.

2. Learning to recognize and manage stress: It's important to identify the signs of stress and take steps to manage it. This might involve taking breaks when needed, practicing deep breathing, or seeking professional help if necessary.

3. Prioritizing rest and relaxation: Getting adequate sleep, taking breaks during the day, and scheduling downtime are important for recharging and preventing burnout. By incorporating these practical strategies into daily lives, self-care can be prioritized, leading to improved emotional well-being and a healthier overall lifestyle.

Key Tips for Enhancing SMEs: Building Resilience & Economic Growth

1. Diversify Suppliers and Customer Bases: Encourage SMEs to expand their networks and explore new markets to reduce reliance on a single supplier or customer. By diversifying, SMEs can mitigate risks and build a more robust supply chain that can adapt to changing circumstances.

2. Embrace Technology and Digital Solutions: SMEs should leverage e-commerce platforms, cloud-based systems, and digital communication tools to streamline operations, access new markets, and enhance efficiency. Implementing innovative technologies enables SMEs to stay agile and competitive in the global market.

3. Focus on Risk Management and Planning: Governments, policymakers, and industry leaders must collaborate to develop supportive policies and risk management frameworks. Proactive planning ensures SMEs have the necessary tools to anticipate and navigate disruptions effectively.

4. Ensure Access to Finance: Tailored financial services and support mechanisms should be provided by governments and financial institutions. Flexible financing options, grants, and business development services empower SMEs to invest in their growth and resilience, strengthening their contributions to the economy.

5. Foster Collaborative Relationships: Encourage collaboration between SMEs and larger enterprises to share resources, knowledge, and expertise. Such partnerships can lead to innovative solutions, foster resilience, and create an environment where SMEs can thrive even in challenging times.

By following these key tips, SMEs can enhance their ability to adapt, build resilient supply chains, and continue driving innovation, job creation, and economic growth.

Another crucial aspect to consider is access to finance. SMEs often face constraints when seeking funding to invest in technology, expand their operations, or withstand economic shocks. Governments and financial institutions need to provide tailored financial services and support mechanisms specifically designed for SMEs. Implementing programs that offer flexible financing options, grants, and business development services can empower SMEs to invest in their growth and resilience.

Prioritizing the resilience of SMEs and building robust supply chains is of utmost importance for economic stability and growth. By adopting proactive measures such as diversification, leveraging technology, and ensuring access to finance, we can safeguard the sustainability of SMEs and strengthen their contributions to the economy. Collaboration between governments, policymakers, industry leaders, and SMEs themselves will be pivotal in creating an environment that fosters resilience and empowers the backbone of our economy. With the right support, SMEs can effectively adapt to global solutions, driving forward progress and overcoming challenges presented by an ever-changing world.creating an environment that fosters resilience and empowers them further.

A LUXURIOUS LAKESIDE RETREAT BLENDING MODERN ELEGANCE WITH RUSTIC CHARM

WRITTEN BY VIKKI JONES

Nestled on the lakeshore, *Chalet Magog, a creation by renowned interior designer Mélodie Violet and her design studio Imagine*, epitomizes natural serenity and modern elegance intertwined with rustic charm. This 280m² chalet offers an immersive forest experience with an optimized layout, large openings to the outdoors, and refined interior details, making it a true ode to tranquility.

The chalet's expansive windows open to breathtaking views, flooding the interior with natural light, showcasing a decor predominantly adorned with wood. The use of maple panels and pine cladding merges modern elegance with the chalet's rustic essence. At its core lies a central fireplace that elegantly separates the cozy living room from the winter garden, creating distinct yet comforting living spaces.

From ingenious storage solutions to elegant furniture, custom fittings have been designed to perfectly meet the needs of a modern family lifestyle. Every detail, from sculptural light fixtures to a soothing color palette, has been meticulously considered, contributing to making this chalet a peaceful and refined retreat, and a true sanctuary in the heart of nature.

The Magog project truly showcases Imagine's expertise in crafting living spaces that exceed expectations, blending modern design with traditional charm. Mélodie Violet has created a space that speaks to the soul, where each element harmonizes to offer moments of life. The Magog chalet is a project that redefines harmony between humans and nature.

PHOTO CREDIT: STUDIO CRBN

POWER & GREATNESS

KNOW YOUR ABILITIES & THE VALUE YOU BRING TO THE TABLE

Written by Vikki Jones

It's easy to overlook the powerful force residing within each of us. The power within you is a gift waiting to be unwrapped, a treasure waiting to be discovered. Our greatness is not predetermined by external factors but lies deep within, awaiting embrace and release.

Realizing our true power and greatness involves shedding self-imposed limitations that hinder reaching our full potential. It's about tapping into an inner reservoir of strength, authenticity, and resilience to navigate life's challenges with confidence. Surrounding ourselves with supportive people who uplift and encourage us is crucial on the journey to self-discovery.

The journey towards greatness begins with a commitment to self-discovery – a process of exploring our talents, strengths, values, and passions to uncover the essence of who we truly are. It entails embracing our authenticity, standing confidently in our truth, and releasing any doubts or fears that may hinder our progress.

I, Vikki Jones, am the visionary behind VMH Publishing, want to remind each of us that the power within us is a gift waiting to be unwrapped, a treasure waiting to be discovered. This notion serves as a catalyst for introspection and self-realization, prompting us to shed self-imposed limitations and embrace the boundless possibilities that await us.

Central to achieving greatness is the cultivation of a strong sense of self-worth and resilience. By affirming our worthiness, nurturing our inner strength, and embracing our unique qualities, we set the stage for transformative growth and empowerment. It is through this process that we learn to navigate external influences with confidence and clarity, guarding our power from forces that seek to diminish our light.

"The power within us is a gift waiting to be unwrapped, a treasure waiting to be discovered.

In the journey towards personal power, it is important to remember that greatness is not defined by external measures of success or the approval of others. Instead, true greatness lies in the ability to cultivate a sense of inner strength, confidence, and authenticity that allows one to shine brightly in a world filled with endless possibilities."

Surrounding ourselves with supportive people who uplift and inspire us is also instrumental in our quest for greatness. Positive relationships and connections can serve as pillars of strength, reinforcing our sense of self-worth and providing a nurturing environment for personal growth and development.

As we embark on the path of self-realization, remember to affirm your worthiness, embrace your authenticity, and boldly step into your true essence. By releasing self-imposed limitations and welcoming boundless possibilities, you open yourself up to transformative growth. Each step taken brings you closer to uncovering the extraordinary aspects that make you unique and powerful.

As we step boldly into our greatness, we are reminded of the importance of living vibrantly and authentically. It is in the moments of self-discovery, in the recognition of our limitless potential, and in the unwavering commitment to shaping our own destiny that we truly flourish. By embracing the brilliance of our true selves and letting it shine forth, we illuminate the path towards our dreams and inspire others to do the same.

To achieve dreams and live a fulfilling life, it's essential to recognize the limitless potential within and harness it with unwavering determination. By nurturing the brilliance of your true self and letting it shine forth, you inspire others to embrace their own greatness. Stand tall in your truth, embrace your inner strength, and remember that the power within you is truly limitless.

Achieving greatness is not a destination but a continuous journey of self-exploration, empowerment, and growth. It requires us to

look within, to recognize our inherent potential, and to step into our power with courage and conviction. May we all embrace the challenge of unlocking our true greatness, knowing that the journey itself is a testament to the extraordinary capacity that resides within each of us. Trust in your power, embrace your greatness, and let your light shine bright for all the world to see.

A Quick How-To Embrace Your True Greatness Guide

Beginning the journey of self-exploration, empowerment, and growth is an ongoing process that allows us to recognize and unlock our true greatness. It requires courage, conviction, and trust in our abilities to step into our power and let our light shine bright.

Step 1: Look Within
To begin the journey towards greatness, take the time to look within yourself. Reflect on your strengths, values, and aspirations. Consider what makes you unique and how you can use your individuality to make a positive impact on the world.

Step 2: Recognize Your Potential
Acknowledge and embrace your inherent potential. Believe in your abilities and the value you bring to the table. Understand that you have the capacity to achieve greatness and make a difference in your own life and the lives of others.

Step 3: Step Into Your Power
Embrace your greatness with courage and conviction. Take proactive steps to cultivate your skills, pursue your passions, and overcome challenges. Trust in your abilities and have faith in the journey ahead.

Step 4: Embrace the Journey
Understand that achieving greatness is not just a destination but a continuous journey. Embrace the challenges and setbacks as opportunities for growth and learning. Embrace the process and remain committed to unlocking your true potential.

Step 5: Let Your Light Shine
As you progress on your journey, let your light shine bright. Share your gifts, talents, and wisdom with the world. Inspire others through your actions and be a beacon of hope and positivity.

AI Can Support Counselors According to New Recommendations

Artificial intelligence (AI) shows promise as a valuable support tool for delivery of mental health services, educational guidance and career counseling. But the American Counseling Association (ACA), the leading organization representing counseling professionals, warns that consumers should not use AI as a substitute for a human counselor.

ACA's AI Working Group has issued a set of guidelines to help counselors and their clients understand the value and limitations of using chatbots, robotics and other nascent AI tools in mental health services. Clients should understand the technical shortcomings, unresolved biases and security risks of AI before using it as part of their counseling, says Russell Fulmer, PhD, LPC, chair of the working group and professor and director of graduate counseling programs at Husson University in Bangor, Maine.

"AI may offer promising benefits, but its claims can sometimes be overly ambitious and simplified, non-evidence based, or even incorrect and potentially harmful," the panel states in its recommendations.

AI technologies are designed to engage in the same reasoning, decision-making and language comprehension of the human mind. Counselors already use them to automate administrative tasks such as reports on a client's progress, says Olivia Uwamahoro Williams, PhD, NCC, LPC, clinical assistant professor of counseling education at the College of William & Mary in Williamsburg, Virginia, and a member of the ACA working group. Some are inviting clients to use AI chatbots to help them understand and manage their thoughts and feelings between therapy sessions, Fulmer says.

But as the ACA panel notes, the algorithms include the same fallibilities and biases of the humans who create them. The AI tools may rely on data that overlook certain communities, particularly marginalized groups, creating the risk of culturally insensitive care. They risk providing false claims or inaccurate information. And although they show promise as a diagnostic aid, they can't replicate the professional reasoning and expertise required to accurately assess an individual's mental health needs. "Unlike human counselors, AI lacks the ability to holistically consider a client's complex personal history, cultural context, and varied symptoms and factors among others," the guidelines state.

"Therefore, while AI can be a supportive tool, it should not replace the professional judgment of professional counselors. It is recommended that AI be used as an adjunct to, rather than a replacement for, the expertise provided by professional counselors." The ACA panel recommends that clients consider the following:

- Make sure your provider informs you about what AI can and cannot offer so you can make informed decisions about using it as part of your counseling.
- To protect confidentiality, verify that the AI tools you use comply with federal and state privacy laws and regulations.
- Discuss with your counselor how to mitigate the risks of AI tools providing falsehoods or factual mistakes that could harm your well-being.
- Refrain from using AI for crisis response, and instead use crisis hotlines, emergency services and other forms of assistance from qualified professionals.

Providers should develop a detailed understanding of AI technologies, their applications in counseling services, and their effects on confidentiality and privacy, the working group says. The recommendations call for counselors to receive comprehensive and continuous training in evolving AI applications, says Fulmer, who studies AI in the behavioral sciences.

"We are ethically obliged before we use something to be quite competent in it," he says. "So, one of our recommendations is to simply accumulate more knowledge about AI."

The panel also calls on technology developers to involve clients and counselors in the design of relevant AI tools. Including these users will ensure that AI tools are client-centered and address real-world needs.

ACA is taking a leadership role in ensuring the appropriate use of AI in mental health services, says Shawn Boynes, FASAE, CAE, the organization's chief executive officer. "The adoption of AI and its impact on mental health is growing exponentially in a variety of ways that we're still trying to understand," Boynes says. "As one of many mental health organizations focused on well-being, we want to lead by offering solutions to help mitigate future concerns."

'The Power Within' is not about finding something new; it's about uncovering something that has always been there."

NEW

ACHIEVE TRUE GREATNESS AND
REMOVE SELF-IMPOSED LIMITATIONS

THE POWER
WITHIN

VIKKI JONES

amazon.com
Walmart
BARNES & NOBLE

ALSO VISIT
VIKKIMJONES.COM

THE 96TH OSCARS
A NIGHT OF GLAMOUR AND CELEBRATION

by Vikki Jones

The 96th Oscars was a night to remember, filled with glitz, glamour, and celebration. The Governors Ball, the official after-party of the Oscars, was a star-studded affair, featuring a menu of delectable dishes and signature cocktails. Pre-events, such as the red carpet arrivals and pre-show performances, set the stage for the evening's festivities, while the audience was treated to memorable moments and heartfelt speeches from the winners. The telecast was filled with highlights, including standout performances and emotional acceptance speeches, making the 96th Oscars a night to remember.

With a membership of more than 10,500 global film industry artists and leaders, an acclaimed film museum and collection, and world-renowned awards for cinematic achievements, the Academy of Motion Picture Arts and Sciences is the home of an expertise and reach that is unparalleled. The Academy recognizes and celebrates all aspects of the film industry and the diverse, talented people who make movies.

Mark Ruffalo and Mahershala Ali during the live ABC telecast of the 96th Oscars® at Dolby® Theatre at Ovation Hollywood on Sunday, March 10, 2024. Credit/ProviderTrae Patton / ©A.M.P.A.S.

Forest Whitaker presents a nominee for Oscar® for Actor in a Leading Role during the live ABC telecast of the 96th Oscars® at the Dolby® Theatre at Ovation Hollywood on Sunday, March 10, 2024. Credit/ProviderTrae Patton / ©A.M.P.A.S.

Oscar® winner Holly Waddington attends the Governors Ball following the live ABC telecast of the 96th Oscars® at the Dolby® Theatre at Ovation Hollywood in Los Angeles, CA, on Sunday, March 10, 2024. Credit/Provider David Nguyen / ©A.M.P.A.S.

Dwayne Johnson arrives on the red carpet of the 96th Oscars® at the Dolby® Theatre at Ovation Hollywood on Sunday, March 10, 2024. Photo Credit: Nick Agro @A.M.P.A.S.

Octavia Spencer and guest arrive on the red carpet of the 96th Oscars® at the Dolby® Theatre at Ovation Hollywood on Sunday, March 10, 2024. Photo Credit Nick Agro @A.M.P.A.S.

Ava DuVernay arrives on the red carpet of the 96th Oscars® at the Dolby® Theatre at Ovation Hollywood on Sunday, March 10, 2024. Photo Credit: Nick Agro @A.M.P.A.S.

Matthew McConaughey at The 96th Oscars® at the Dolby® Theatre at Ovation Hollywood on Sunday, March 10, 2024. Credit: Nick Agro @A.M.P.A.S.

The 96th Oscars was a night to remember,
celebrating the best of the film industry.
The audience was treated to memorable moments
and heartfelt speeches from the winners, while the
telecast was filled with highlights, including standout
performances and emotional acceptance speeches.

Oscar® nominees Danielle Brooks, Fred Berner, and Steven Spielberg at the 96th Oscars® at the Dolby® Theatre at Ovation Hollywood on Sunday, March 10, 2024. Photo Credit: Richard Harbaugh @A.M.P.A.S.

Oscar® nominee Paul Giamatti and Elizabeth Cohen at the 96th Oscars® at the Dolby® Theatre at Ovation Hollywood on Sunday, March 10, 2024. Photos Credit: Richard Harbaugh @A.M.P.A.S.

Oscar® nominee Cillian Murphy arrives on the red carpet of the 96th Oscars® at the Dolby® Theatre at Ovation Hollywood on Sunday, March 10, 2024. Photo Credit: Mike Baker / @A.M.P.A.S.

Regina King and Angela Bassett at the 14th Governors Awards in the Ray Dolby Ballroom at Ovation Hollywood on Tuesday, January 9, 2024 Credit: Warrick Page / @ A.M.P.A.S

Jennifer Lawrence arrives on the red carpet of the 96th Oscars® at the Dolby® Theatre at Ovation Hollywood on Sunday, March 10, 2024. Photo Credit: Nick Agro @A.M.P.A.S.

PROMOTE YOUR BUSINESS, BRAND, OR PRODUCTS WITH US AT VMH MAGAZINE!

Are you looking to reach a wider audience and increase your brand visibility? Look no further than VMH Magazine, where we provide various packages to help you showcase your business and products effectively.

Benefits of Advertising with VMH Magazine:

- Reach a diverse and engaged audience of readers
- Increase brand awareness and recognition
- Feature your products in a reputable publication
- Tailored advertising packages to suit your needs
- Access to multiple platforms for maximum exposure

Don't miss the opportunity to elevate your business with VMH Magazine. Contact us today to discuss our advertising packages and take your brand to new heights!

www.vmhmagazine.com

Whether you're a reader seeking an enthralling narrative, an aspiring author yearning to be discovered, or a literary enthusiast eager to explore new horizons, VMH Publishing invites you to embark on a journey of literary discovery. Immerse yourself in thought-provoking stories, poetic prose, and insightful non-fiction that will leave an indelible mark on your mind and heart.

Visit our website, www.vmhpublishing.com, to explore our captivating catalog and join us in our mission to celebrate the power of words. Together, let's redefine literary excellence and shape the future of literature.

The Governors Ball Press Preview for the
96th Oscars® at Ovation Hollywood on
Tuesday, March 5, 2024. The 96th Oscars will
air on Sunday, March 10, 2024 live on ABC.
Credit: Richard Harbaugh / ©A.M.P.A.S.

Prince Robert de Luxembourg, Domaine Clarence Dillon, Wolfgang Puck, Master Chef and Byron Lazaroff-Puck at the Governors Ball Press Preview for the 96th Oscars® at Ovation Hollywood on Tuesday, March 5, 2024. The 96th Oscars will air on Sunday, March 10, 2024 live on ABC. Photo Credit/Al Seib / ©A.M.P.A.S.

Wolfgang Puck: Mastering Culinary Excellence at the Oscars Governors Ball

Written by Vikki Jones

For three decades, Wolfgang Puck has curated the culinary experience at the Oscars Governors Ball, setting a standard of excellence unmatched in the film and entertainment industry. The success of Puck's tenure at this prestigious event highlights essential lessons for businesses aiming for long-term success.

Puck's ability to consistently deliver sophistication, elegance, and top-notch culinary creations at the Oscars showcases his understanding that a dining experience is not just about taste, but about the complete package. Presentation, ambiance, and attention to detail are key elements in creating a memorable experience that goes beyond just the menu.

Sustainability has been a cornerstone of Puck's approach, demonstrating that maintaining high quality doesn't have to come at the cost of the environment. By embracing sustainable practices like sourcing local and organic ingredients and minimizing waste, Puck showcases how businesses can prioritize quality.

Wolfgang Puck arrives on the red carpet of the 96th Oscars® at the Dolby® Theatre at Ovation Hollywood on Sunday, March 10, 2024. Credit Mike Baker / ©A.M.P.A.S.

The 30-year retention of Puck as the caterer for the Oscars underscores his exceptional ability to consistently exceed client expectations. This level of trust and loyalty from clients speaks volumes about the quality of Puck's work and the relationships he has built over the years.

Innovation has been a driving force behind Puck's sustained success. To stay relevant for three decades at such a high-profile event, Puck has continuously pushed boundaries, experimented with new flavors and techniques, and stayed ahead of culinary trends. This commitment to innovation has allowed him to evolve and adapt while delivering exceptional experiences year after year.

Puck's 30-year tenure as the caterer for the Oscars Governors Ball is a testament to his unwavering passion for food and his commitment to delivering exceptional culinary experiences. The 24 karat gold-dusted Oscars desserts and the meticulously curated menu are just a few examples of Puck's dedication to pushing the boundaries of traditional cuisine and creating a truly unforgettable dining experience for the Hollywood elite.

Wolfgang Puck Catering curated an exceptional menu for the Governors Ball, the esteemed celebration following the 96th Oscars awards. Guests had the opportunity to explore five themed stations, each offering a unique culinary experience.

Chicken Pot Pie

Cacio e Pepe Macaroni and Cheese

Highlights from the menu included the delectable Fish & Chips, the enticing Crispy Rice Bar, the tantalizing Chinois On Main, wood-fired pizzas, and the Bar de Pastoreo y Paella featuring Spanish delicacies such as potato omelet with romesco sauce, paellas, and an assortment of desserts.

The menu, prepared by a dedicated team of 120 kitchen professionals, boasted over 60 meticulously crafted dishes and desserts, ranging from classic confections to innovative creations. To top it all off, winners, nominees, and attendees were presented with miniature Oscar "statuette" chocolates, adding a touch of glamour.

Wolfgang Puck, Master Chef, and Byron
Lazaroff-Puck at the Governors Ball Press
Preview for the 96th Oscars® at Ovation
Hollywood on Tuesday, March 5, 2024. The
96th Oscars will air on Sunday, March 10,
Credit/Provider Al Seib / ©A.M.P.A.S.

(Family Features) Between work, family obligations and a constantly changing world, people in the United States are stressed. In fact, U.S. workers are among the most stressed in the world, according to a State of the Global Workplace study. While some stress is unavoidable and can be good for you, constant or chronic stress can have real consequences for your mental and physical health.

Chronic stress can increase your lifetime risk of heart disease and stroke. It can also lead to unhealthy habits like overeating, physical inactivity and smoking while also increasing risk factors, including high blood pressure, depression and anxiety. However, a scientific statement from the American Heart Association shows reducing stress and cultivating a positive mindset can improve health and well-being.

To help people understand the connection between stress and physical health, the American Heart Association offers these science-backed insights to help reduce chronic stress.

Stay Active
Exercise is one of the easiest ways to keep your body healthy and release stress. Physical activity is linked to lower risk of diseases, stronger bones and muscles, improved mental health and cognitive function and lower risk of depression. It can also help increase energy and improve quality of sleep. The American Heart Association recommends adults get at least 150 minutes per week of moderate-intensity activity, 75 minutes of vigorous activity or a combination.

Meditate
Incorporate meditation and mindfulness practices into your day to give yourself a few minutes to create some distance from daily stress. Some studies show meditation can reduce blood pressure, improve sleep, support the immune system and increase your ability to process information.

Practice Positivity
A positive mindset can improve overall health. Studies show a positive mindset can help you live longer, and happy individuals tend to sleep better, exercise more, eat better and not smoke. Practice

5 HEALTHY HABITS TO HELP REDUCE STRESS

positive self-talk to help you stay calm. Instead of saying, "everything is going wrong," re-frame the situation and remind yourself "I can handle this if I take it one step at a time."

Show Gratitude
Gratitude – or thankfulness – is a powerful tool that can reduce levels of depression and anxiety and improve sleep. Start by simply writing down three things you're grateful for each day.

Find a Furry Friend
Having a pet may help you get more fit; lower stress, blood pressure, cholesterol and blood sugar; and boost overall happiness and well-being. When you see, touch, hear or talk to companion animals, you may feel a sense of goodwill, joy, nurturing and happiness. At the same time, stress hormones are suppressed. Dog ownership is also associated with a lower risk of depression, according to research published by the American Heart Association.

Find more stress-management tips at Heart.org/stress.

Stress 101

Understanding stress is an important step in managing and reducing it. Consider these things to know about stress and how it could affect your life:

- Today, 1 in 3 adults in the U.S. report being worried or depressed.
- Higher levels of the stress hormone cortisol are linked to increased risk of high blood pressure and cardiovascular events like heart disease and stroke.
- The top sources of stress are money, work, family responsibilities and health concerns.
- Work-related stress is associated with a 40% increased risk of cardiovascular disease like heart attack and stroke.

Timing for Success: Mastering the Art of Achieving Goals

Written by Vikki Jones

Timing is a critical element when it comes to achieving success and reaching our goals. Just like a well-choreographed dance, being in sync with the right moment can make all the difference. It's not just about working hard or having a solid plan: it's about understanding when to take action, when to pivot, and when to seize opportunities. Recognizing the importance of timing and mastering its art can significantly enhance our chances of success.

One key aspect of timing for success is knowing when to start. Oftentimes, we may find ourselves waiting for the perfect moment, waiting for all the stars to align. However, it's important to remember that waiting for the ideal conditions can lead to missed opportunities. Instead, we should focus on taking that initial step and starting towards our goals. As the saying goes, "The best time to plant a tree was 20 years ago. The second best time is now." By taking action and starting, we set ourselves on the path to success.

However, timing is not just about starting; it's also about recognizing when to make adjustments. As we progress towards our goals, we may encounter obstacles or unforeseen circumstances. Being able to adapt and adjust our strategies is crucial. Sometimes, it's about being patient and allowing things to unfold naturally. Other times, it's about making bold and timely decisions to steer ourselves back on track. The ability to assess the situation, gauge the right moment, and make necessary adjustments can be a game-changer in achieving our goals. Timing also plays a significant role in seizing opportunities. Opportunities often present themselves unexpectedly, and it's up to us to recognize them and act swiftly. This requires being alert, staying informed, and having a clear vision of our goals. By staying attuned to our surroundings and having a proactive mindset, we position ourselves to capitalize on these opportunities when they arise. As the saying goes, "Luck is what happens when preparation meets opportunity." By being prepared and having a keen sense of timing, we can create our own luck and open doors to success.

Furthermore, timing is closely tied to perseverance. Sometimes, success doesn't come overnight, and it requires patience and persistence. It's important to understand that

timing is not always within our control. There may be setbacks and delays along the way. However, by maintaining our focus, staying committed, and continuously working towards our goals, we position ourselves to be ready for the right moment when it arrives. Timing and perseverance go hand in hand, and together, they can propel us towards our desired outcomes.

To master the art of timing for success, it's crucial to develop self-awareness and intuition. Paying attention to our instincts and inner voice can provide valuable insights into when to take action, when to adjust our strategies, and when to seize opportunities. Additionally, learning from past experiences and observing successful individuals in our fields can provide valuable lessons and guidance on how to navigate timing effectively.

By mastering the art of timing, we can enhance our chances of success and set ourselves on the path to realizing our dreams.

COMFORTABLE
CARRYING OPTIONS

Say goodbye to uncomfortable bags. Vikki Jones' designs prioritize comfort, with padded straps, ergonomic handles, and lightweight construction, ensuring a comfortable carrying experience even during long journeys.

Need extra space? Jones' bags feature expandable compartments, allowing you to increase the capacity when needed. Travel with confidence, knowing you have room for souvenirs or extra work documents.

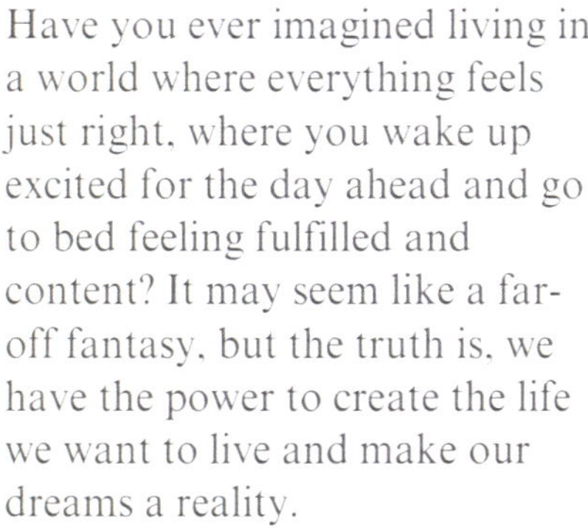

Creating the Life You Want to Live: Manifesting Your Dream Life

Written by Vikki Jones

Have you ever imagined living in a world where everything feels just right, where you wake up excited for the day ahead and go to bed feeling fulfilled and content? It may seem like a far-off fantasy, but the truth is, we have the power to create the life we want to live and make our dreams a reality.

Creating the world you want to live in starts with a clear vision of what you want. Take some time to reflect on your deepest desires and aspirations. What kind of career do you want? What kind of relationships do you want to have? How do you want to feel on a daily basis? Once you have a clear picture of your ideal life, it's time to start taking action to make it happen.

One of the most important steps in creating the world you want to live in is to believe in yourself and your ability to manifest your dreams. This may sound cliché, but the power of positive thinking and belief in yourself is truly transformative. When you believe in your ability to create the life you want, you will naturally start taking the necessary steps to make it happen.

Another key aspect of creating the world you want to live in is to surround yourself with the right people. Your environment and the people you spend time with have a huge impact on your mindset and overall well-being. Surround yourself with positive, supportive, and like-minded ndividuals who share your vision and can help you on your journey.

It's also important to take consistent action towards your goals. Whether it's pursuing further education, networking, or simply taking small steps every day, it's crucial to keep moving forward. Remember, creating the world you want to live in is a journey, not a destination. Be patient with yourself and stay committed to your vision.

Lastly, don't be afraid to dream big and think outside the box. The world we live in is constantly changing, and there are endless possibilities for creating a life that is truly fulfilling and aligned with your values. Don't limit yourself to what you think is possible based on your current circumstances. Dare to dream and pursue your passions with courage and determination.

Creating the world you want to live in is entirely possible. By envisioning your ideal life, believing in yourself, surrounding yourself with the right people, taking consistent action, and daring to dream big, you can make your dreams a reality. So, go ahead and start creating the world you want to live in – the life you've always dreamed of is within your reach.

VMH
Publishing

ARE READY TO WRITE YOUR BOOK

———

WRITING A BOOK IS A TRANSFORMATIVE ENDEAVOR THAT CAN OPEN DOORS TO A MULTITUDE OF NEW BUSINESS OPPORTUNITIES.

The world of literature is a vast and captivating realm that allows authors to share their unique perspectives, stories, and knowledge with readers across the globe. If you've ever felt the burning desire to write a book, now is the perfect time to embark on your authorial journey. In this article, we'll explore the excitement, challenges, and rewards that come with writing a book. So, are you ready to dive into the realm of words and create a masterpiece of your own?

Unleashing Your Creativity:
Writing a book is a powerful outlet for your creativity. It allows you to express your thoughts, emotions, and experiences in a way that resonates with readers. Whether you have a fictional tale brewing in your mind or a non-fiction book idea that can enlighten others, the act of writing enables you to let your imagination soar and bring your ideas to life.

Finding Your Writing Process:
Discovering your unique writing process is a crucial step in the journey of writing a book. Some authors thrive in organized environments, meticulously outlining their chapters and characters before diving into the writing process. Others prefer a more spontaneous approach, allowing the story to unfold naturally as they write.

Overcoming Challenges:
Writing a book is not without its challenges. It requires discipline, dedication, and perseverance. Writer's block, self-doubt, and time management can all pose obstacles along the way. However, by adopting strategies such as setting writing goals, creating a writing routine, and seeking support from writing communities, you can overcome these challenges and keep your creative momentum flowing.

Writing is a powerful tool for communication, bridging gaps and connecting people across time and space. Whether you're sharing stories, ideas, or knowledge, writing allows you to convey your message with clarity and precision. Through your words, you can touch the hearts and minds of readers.

Crafting Memorable Characters and Engaging Plots:
One of the most thrilling aspects of writing a book is the opportunity to create memorable characters and captivating plots. Dive deep into character development, breathing life into your protagonists and antagonists. Craft a compelling plot that keeps readers turning pages, eager to unravel the twists and turns of your story. With each word, you have the power to transport readers to new worlds and evoke emotions that linger long after the final page.

Navigating the Publishing Landscape:
Once your manuscript is complete, the next step is to navigate the publishing landscape. Traditional publishing, self-publishing, and hybrid publishing are all viable options, each with its own advantages and considerations. Research the different paths, weigh the pros and cons, and choose the publishing route that aligns with your goals and aspirations as an author.

Sharing Your Book with the World:
Publishing your book is just the beginning. The joy of writing is in sharing your creation with the world. Engage in book launches, author readings, and literary events to connect with readers and build your author brand. Leverage the power of social media and online platforms to expand your reach and engage with a global audience. Embrace the feedback and reviews, as they provide valuable insights and fuel your growth as an author.

Embarking on the journey of writing a book is an exhilarating endeavor that opens doors to endless possibilities. It allows you to leave a lasting impact on readers, share your unique voice, and contribute to the rich tapestry of literature. So, are you ready to embrace your authorial journey? Grab your pen, unleash your creativity, and let the words flow onto the pages. Your book awaits, and the world is ready to be captivated by your story.